D1228431

edge of the ocean

LIVING
NATURE
SERIES

574.526
W1

By William White, Jr., Ph.D.

PHOTOGRAPHS BY THE AUTHOR

 STERLING PUBLISHING CO., INC. NEW YORK

Oak Tree Press Co., Ltd. London & Sydney

MADISON COUNTY -
CANTON PUBLIC LIBRARY SYSTEM
CANTON, MISS. 39046

OTHER BOOKS BY THE SAME AUTHOR

American Chameleon

The Angelfish: Its Life Cycle

Cycle of the Seasons

Earthworm Is Born

Edge of the Pond

Forest and Garden

Frog Is Born

The Guppy: Its Life Cycle

The Siamese Fighting Fish: Its Life Cycle

Turtle Is Born

Acknowledgements

The author and publisher wish to thank the officers of the firm of Wild-Heerbrugg, Heerbrugg, Switzerland, Dr. Ralph Gander, Mr. Walter Wittweiler and Mr. Walter Gumpertz, for the use of their new Photomakroskop M 400 for the microphotographs and macrophotographs in this book; Mr. Robert Tuten and Mr. Rudy Lewis for the use of several seashore scenes; William White III and James M. White for their help in developing special study apparatus; and Rebecca L. White and Sara A. White for preparing the manuscript.

Copyright © 1977 by Sterling Publishing Co., Inc.
Two Park Avenue, New York, N.Y. 10016
Distributed in Australia and New Zealand by Oak Tree Press Co., Ltd.,
P.O. Box J34, Brickfield Hill, Sydney 2000, N.S.W.
Distributed in the United Kingdom and elsewhere in the British Commonwealth
by Ward Lock Ltd., 116 Baker Street, London W 1
Manufactured in the United States of America
All rights reserved
Library of Congress Catalog Card No.: 77-080953
Sterling ISBN 0-8069-3582-0 Trade   Oak Tree 7061-2563-0
3583-9 Library

Contents

Color section follows page 32

On many beaches all of the zones from the high grassy dunes to the submerged zone can be easily seen at a glance.

Introduction

Over 70 per cent of the earth's surface is covered by the salt water of the ocean, the vast interconnected mass of seas surrounding the continents. The ocean has many edges and it forms a number of different zones where it touches the land. These edges are the interfaces where land, sea and air all meet and influence each other. These interfaces and the areas around them are among the most vital and diverse environments on the surface of the earth.

The continents are surrounded by submerged zones called continental shelves. These shelves vary in width—they may be so narrow as to be virtually non-existent, or they may reach a width of 930 miles (1,500 km), as along the Arctic coast of Siberia. However, the average width of the shelves is 48 miles (78 km). The point where the shelf drops off into the ocean depths is called the shelf break, and may vary from 66 to 1,800 feet (20 to 550 metres) in depth.

The water of the continental shelf is very rich in minerals brought down from the land by streams and rivers. Along the continental side of the shelf, the

Anyone, no matter how young, can be a successful beachcomber. However, a good net and a plastic collecting bag can add interest to a walk at low tide.

coastlands have been, and are still being, formed, including some of their best known features—the coastal wetlands and the broad, sandy beaches. Nearly everywhere in the world where there are beaches, people of all ages enjoy them. Major fishing, boating and vacation areas throughout the world are to be found along such beaches. It is easy to discover a great deal about the edges of the ocean by walking along the beach or wading or rowing through the wetlands, and observing the signs of natural forces all around. All you need are a swimsuit, rubber boots, a net and the curiosity to go and look.

The Many-Edged Ocean

The ocean has three main edges or interfaces, which we shall refer to as the *landside,* the *waterside* and the *airside.* The largest and easiest to observe is the landside. There are really two main types of landsides. The first is the sandy beach where the ocean washes in over the land and the tides rise and recede twice each day.

The Beach

The beach is a type of landside marked by a number of zones, each created by tidal action. The highest and driest is the dune zone, where the sand is piled in banks and hillocks. Here low shrubs and bushes, as well as salt-resistant grasses, grow and help to hold the sand in place against the wind. Below the dunes and within the region occasionally covered by the salt water are a number of beach zones. These may be so hard to differentiate that they seem to be one huge flat sand plane. However, the force of the tide actually does divide the broadest and the flattest beach into zones. The main zones—the upper,

The wide sand beach contains many zones and environments for specialized organisms and is littered with plants and the remains of animals at low tide.

middle and lower beach—each have a different degree of wetness, and other factors, as we shall see later.

The constant surging inland of the ocean can erode away great quantities of sand and rock and just as easily deposit it again at another location. The grinding action of the surf pulverizes stones and shells along the beach reducing them to sand. Sand is thus the last stage of the breakdown of rocks and minerals.

Since water holds heat longer than air, the ocean controls the temperature and the climate along the shore. The salt air kills many types of trees and shrubs—so the ocean

A tiny wind-blown pine aids in anchoring the dune sand against erosion.

actually controls the kinds of plants that can grow on the landside. The landside is usually windblown and subject to being flooded. If the region is one where hurricanes or violent winter storms occur, flooding may occasionally extend many miles inland. In this way, a wide strip of land along the coast may actually be formed by the ocean.

Not only the physical form of the land, but also the plants and animals are affected by the sea. Plants must be salt-resistant and capable of growing strong roots to stay in place and to resist wind erosion. The animal life is even more affected, since the chief supply of food comes from the ocean. While all of the components—land, water, and air—interreact with each other, it is the sea which is dominant.

The overwhelming mass of life forms at the ocean's edge consists of invertebrates. Of these, shell animals—bivalves and crustaceans, which are found much less abundantly in fresh-water lakes and ponds, predominate. The crab is the great scavenger of the beach and coastal swamp, taking the place of the mammals and reptiles which thrive farther inland. The birds, which are especially numerous, are all adapted to swimming and feeding in the shallow waters. They have special internal systems which allow them to drink salt water and to eat the strong, salty flesh of clams, crabs, and fishes. Many of the birds that nest in the dunes actually secrete large amounts of salt through glands in the head to keep the internal salt in their muscles and blood below that of the ocean water which they swallow.

The Wetlands or Estuarine Side

The second type of landside is that of the estuary, the point where rivers drain into the sea. This is the meeting place where mineral-laden waters from the land mix with the ocean water washing up with each high tide. The

The herring gull is one of the most common of all shore birds, swooping and zooming over the wave tops and running along the shores.

The mudbanks and estuarine channels provide miles of small canals where fish and crabs are abundant.

A long channel in an estuary is lined with swampy vegetation growing right to the water's edge.

The roots of the grasses are above water twice daily as the tide recedes from the wetlands.

The mudbank with its thick crop of grasses.

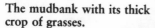

The incoming tide washes a deep channel between the stands of reeds along the estuary.

estuarine environment is always flooded. Here the temperature, salinity (salt content of the water) and other physical characteristics are likely to undergo extremes. The water washing any one spot may be nearly fresh at one time of the day and almost totally salt at another. The temperature may be fairly warm at high tide, as the warm ocean water flows in, and very cold at low tide when the shallow fresh water is cooled by the wind.

The effects of the tide on the estuary are much less than along the sandy beach. The estuarine bottom is usually mud, or gravel mixed with mud, and is matted with thick growths of emergent plants, that is, land plants whose roots are in shallow water. Wide lagoons occur, filled

Whole colonies of invertebrates thrive in the holes along the open mudbanks. They withdraw during low tide and feed heavily at high tide.

with shallow water that is half salt and half fresh. Such a mixture, called brackish water, supports an enormous variety of microscopic and larger forms of life. The estuarine environment has been called the "nursery of the sea," because vast numbers of young invertebrates and fishes hatch and pass the earliest stages of their life cycles in it.

The mud banks of the estuary swarm with insects. One of the most common is the mosquito—myriads of its waterborne larvae are eaten by young fishes. The emergent plants and their submerged roots act just as do the

The shoots of salt-resistant bog plants appear through the wetland mud.

emergent plants of the fresh-water pond—they catch and hold the soil until larger dry-land plants can become established and the lagoon ultimately becomes dry land.

The wet mud supports a mixture of plant types and dozens of species of the larger invertebrates. Even a hole only 2 or 4 inches (5 or 10 centimetres) below the surface of the bank may be filled with water and is therefore a nearly perfect habitat for a crab or worm. At some distance back from the water's edge there usually are many small ponds, which are choked with algae and crawling with tiny invertebrates. Here, the turtle reigns supreme.

15

Tiny pools of remaining brackish water are choked with algae at low tide. Careful examination will uncover the young of fish and immature forms of invertebrates in such pools.

The large bays and lagoons of the estuary have low banks often totally submerged at high tide, but farther inland the rivers and streams have higher banks. Here trees grow as the final wave of succession. Succession is the name given to the process by which wetlands and ponds become dry land as different types of land plants succeed one another. However, most tree species are discouraged from taking over the areas occupied by lower-growing plants, because they cannot tolerate the presence of so much salt in the soil where these plants grow.

Both the sandy beach and the estuarine banks support a very large population of birds. The evidence of their

Farther up into the wetlands, narrow streams bring fresh water dark with pine and cedar sap to the estuary. Only a few steps beyond the reeds, the trees of a wood appear.

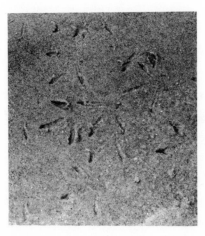

Both the ocean side and the estuarine side of the ocean shore are homes for millions of birds. The beach is sprinkled with the footprints of small birds following the tide line along the shore.

The long bill of the oyster-catcher is used for feeding in the soft bottom, which it sifts for invertebrates.

continual foraging for food is everywhere. Some species are filter feeders, that is, they sift the sand and mud for invertebrates and tiny fishes, which they eat at a prodigious rate. Others are scavengers, cleaning up the clams, crabs, and fishes trapped in shallow water or left dead on the beach by the rush of the tide.

The Ocean

Just as the landside exists in two different forms—the ocean and the estuarine—so does the waterside itself. These forms are the ocean and again the estuarine.

As we have seen, the oceanside has a characteristic series of zones from the dunes through an upper and middle beach to a lower beach which is only occasionally

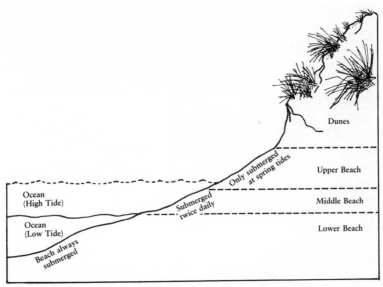

Diagram A. Beach Zones

dry. (Diagram A) This beach is continually being built up and washed away by the surging and undertow of the surf and tides. If you look, you can see that the sand is sweeping about tiny objects such as clam shells, and you can watch small invertebrates as they swim continually in and out with the currents.

The two daily extremes of the tides are called the high or *flood* tide when the water is highest on the beach and the low or *ebb* tide when the water is lowest on the beach. At low tide, large areas of sand are left uncovered and vast numbers of shore birds then forage the sand for their food.

The surface of the water is blown by the wind at high tide in a marsh
by the estuary.

This food consists mainly of invertebrates, particularly molluscs. The molluscs, mostly bivalves such as clams and mussels, filter microscopic life from the ocean as their food, before they, in turn, become the food of shore birds. Thus, the presence of huge populations of shore birds is due ultimately to the abundance of microscopic food in the sea.

The very saltiness of the ocean water provides the necessary materials for microscopic plants to grow. These then are eaten by thousands of species of animals from microscopic zooplankton to the largest clams.

While the ocean cannot hold as much dissolved oxygen as fresh water (about 20 per cent less under the best conditions), it contains enormous amounts of dissolved minerals, many of them salts. The amounts of salt and dissolved oxygen vary greatly from the waters of the oceanside to those of the estuarine. At times during periods of especially low water level, the water from areas where oak or cedar trees grow will drain into the estuaries carrying a red-brown stain and a strong sap-like smell from the trees. Locally called cedar water, it produces and supports a special group of microorganisms.

Minerals

The streams and rivers formed by the runoff of snow and rain have been carrying minerals from the land into the seas for millions of years. The ocean water holds these substances in solution. They are there in great abundance

A peaceful scene by a stream flowing through the reeds to the estuary on a hot summer day. Mosquitoes and other water-hatched insects arise by the billions from such quiet streams.

to be utilized by plants and animals. The most important, in order of abundance, are various compounds of chlorine, sodium, sulphur, magnesium, calcium, potassium, bromine, carbon and strontium.

Some chemicals are in such small quantities that they are nearly impossible to detect, yet various plants and animals extract and use them in certain biological functions. Thus plants extract phosphates, nitrates, iron,

The emergent plants along the estuary are the refuges for many invertebrates which filter their microscopic food from the flowing water.

cobalt, manganese, copper and zinc. Animals of various species are known to extract manganese, copper, zinc, phosphorus and vanadium.

There are also appreciable quantities of other elements less often, or rarely ever, used by living creatures, such as silicon, iodine, silver and gold.

Estuarine Water

The continually advancing tide brings these minerals as high as the upper beach where they are available to algae and invertebrates. But it is in the estuarine waters where the algae flourish and invertebrates are most

Large invertebrates, such as this crab, forage along the quiet margins of the estuary. Many species are fully capable of leaving the water for extended periods to eat animal materials which they find along the shore.

numerous. The estuarine water contains dissolved minerals and is called "hard" because of this mineral content. The richness of the estuarine waters provides food for one of the larger invertebrates, the crab. In fresh-water ponds, the frog is the aquatic creature in the environment that

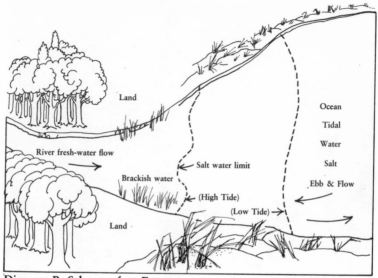

Diagram B. Scheme of an Estuary

preys chiefly on insects and other invertebrates. In the estuary this place is taken by the crab, which eats virtually any available food living or dead.

The estuarine area is also known as the "wetlands," a term specifically applied to the very shallow mud flats lying back of the lagoons and bays. The scheme of the estuary can be seen in many coastal maps where there are numerous inlets and bays at the mouths of rivers and streams. (Diagram B)

The incoming tide tends to carry in sand from the deeper sea bed while the outgoing tide tends to extract mud and silt from the estuary and carry it out to the ocean-

Like the ocean side, the estuary has its landside also. It is made up of these large expanses of swamp grasses and low shrubs growing on the salt marsh.

side. Depending on the degree to which one effect outweighs the other, either the sandy beach or the mud flat may increase or decrease over a period of years.

Acidity and Alkalinity

The estuarine water has the same minerals in it in solution as the ocean but in much lower concentrations. In chemistry, the symbol "pH" is a number that shows the concentration of hydrogen ions (H+) and hydroxyl (OH—) ions and thus the degree of acidity or alkalinity of the water. This degree is of great importance, as it in-

A high pressure flow of water runs through a narrow opening into the salt marshes of the wetlands as the tide comes in.

fluences the amount and type of minerals found in the water and affects the movement, respiration and internal chemistry of all life within the environment. The neutral pH occurs where the concentration of H+ (acid) and OH— (base) are equal, and the number expressing this is 7. The range from 0–7 is acid and from 7–14, the top number on the scale, is alkaline or base.

Ocean water is virtually always basic and may vary from 7.1 to 9 or above. The water of estuaries on the other hand may range as low as 5.3, which is very acid. It seems that most fish eggs and invertebrates thrive best between 6.7, slightly acid, and 8.7, slightly basic. The body

The salt-tolerant plants on the mud flats of the estuary are only washed at high tide.

fluids of many sea species are often very slightly more acid than the water surrounding them.

Salinity

Another important measure applied to sea water is the salinity, or salt content. The salt content of the oceans of the world is less where there are inflows of fresh water from river systems. The salinity of large bays can be markedly less than that of the open sea. The salinity of brackish water varies with the degree of mixing caused by the incoming tides, and often large lagoons and bays can have a very low degree of salinity. Fish and invertebrate

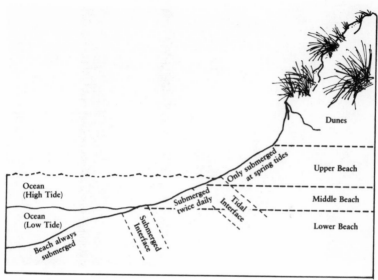

Diagram C. Beach Biozones

species living in brackish water can usually withstand such changes and many thousands of species of fish hatch and grow in one state of salinity, mature and feed in a much higher salinity, and return to the lower salinity to spawn. Two large food fishes, the salmon and the shad, do this year after year.

The Beach Zones

The ocean portion of the waterside is the easiest edge of the ocean to find and observe. While it appears continuous, it is actually divided into a number of specific zones. These are the different zones covered by the water to different depths. (Diagram C) The beach zones each

Occasionally small fishes will be trapped in the middle beach or dead ones will wash in. They are quickly found and eaten by the watchful gulls.

have specific communities of living creatures so they are more than just water zones, they are *biozones*. There are basically four biozones—the dunes and inland area, and the upper, middle and lower beach. The dunes, virtually never covered by water except during hurricanes, are inhabited by mice, some reptiles and the huge population of birds already mentioned.

The upper beach just below the dunes is usually dry. The belt farthest away from the water is called the *berm* and marks the limit of the upper beach. Wind is as much responsible for erosion of the berm as is the water. The upper beach is flooded twice a day at high tide. The animal and plant community of the upper beach can resist flooding, although the inhabitants are adapted to breathing air and living on land. Of the beach

Rocks which lie along the beach within the sweep of the tide support whole colonies of animals and plants which hide among the crevices and dark pools at low tide.

communities, this one is the least dependent on food brought in by tidal action.

The middle beach is exposed to the air only twice a day at low tide. Here, the animal and plant community is able to resist drying and many of the invertebrates can bury in the soft sand below the water level to stay moist. Many of the middle beach species absorb oxygen from the sea water and are really aquatic species adapted to resist temporary drying in air. Few can resist direct exposure to sunlight.

A large rock, a depression or even a man-made piling will provide a special environment. Around and beneath

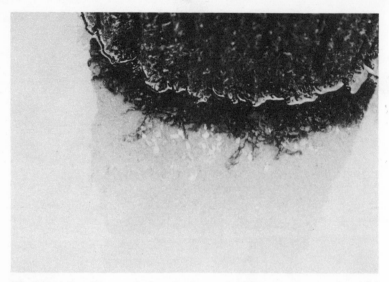

The base of a piling sunk deep in the sand makes a very extensive tidal environment. The crevices and tiny holes in the wood are homes for many types of marine worms and barnacles. The fringe of algae around the base provides hiding places for shrimps and tiny crabs and the soft sand at the base often covers the eggs and young of fish species. The author extracted 9 species of invertebrates, 4 species of fishes and several kinds of algae, all from this one piling pool area at low tide.

such objects, tide pools form, where whole communities of plants and animals can survive the tidal surges.

The Airside

The airside is the last of the three primary interfaces, which together constitute the coastal environment. The wind, made turbulent by the heating and cooling effect of the ocean, can shift masses of sand and enormous quantities of water. The plants which grow on the wind-swept

The sun rises over the wetlands with the shoreline in the distance.

The blue-claw crab is king of the estuary.

(Above) A large growth of
lichens flourishes in the salt
air of the landside.
(Right) A large heron watches
for food or danger in the marsh.

B

Grain is thrown on the ice and snow to feed the starving wild fowl.

White barnacles above and black mussels below cling to a piling at low tide.

C

Large gulls sleep on the rocks above the upper beach.

A fresh-water stream flows out from among pines and bog plants into the estuary.

The innermost portion of the beach is the dunes. The hills of sand are subject to massive erosion by the wind and shifting by the exceptionally high winter tides when coastal storms whip the waves as high as 30 feet (9 metres) and send them inland, overwhelming the shore. The dune area is an invaluable environment for shore birds and many species of plants and invertebrates.

dunes must either bend easily with the shifting winds or be low and deeply rooted to resist the onslaught of the wind.

The birds of the coastal regions are strong fliers who utilize the wind currents in flight. An abundance of food

The wide variety of plants growing over the dunes in this well-protected animal sanctuary offers food and protection for many species of birds. The author counted well over one hundred bird nests in less than an acre of ground, many around the yaupon, bayberry and sandbur plants.

and an expanse of unobstructed flyways have made the shore birds very prolific. Not only are a good number of species found on most coasts, but there are large populations of most species.

The crowns of grasses growing here are holding the sand against the wind. However, in the sand below the dune (upper right) the tracks of the very destructive dune-buggies can be seen. While providing joy rides for vacationers, these vehicles permanently destroy the ocean environments.

Erosion

The grasses are all-important to the continuation of the sandy beach ecology. They are the first wall of security against wind erosion and in places where they die out or are plowed or run down, severe erosion always results. The winter storms often send the high tides in much farther, farther than the normal flow. Such very high floods leave behind large piles of shells and other debris. These are soon picked over by the crabs and beach insects that dwell in dry sand. The wind and the ocean work

35

The highest water mark of the winter storms is always marked by large numbers of shells washed high on the beach. These clam shells have all been broken open by gulls that ate the contents, after which tidal action ground the shells to shards on the sand. The broken shells are washed far inland by winter winds, high tides and trapped by sand gullies.

together as well as against each other always at the expense of the land. The landside is very changeable and may be altered continually by the wind and water working upon it.

Life Forms of the Middle Beach

A walk along the beach will reveal many different species of wildlife. Some look like plants but are actually animals of types not found on land and only rarely and in much reduced size in fresh water.

One of the most highly adapted groups are the barnacles. These are actually sedentary crustaceans related to the free-swimming lobsters and shrimps. They usually become attached to fixed objects such as rocks or pilings or to moving objects such as ship bottoms and even whales, tortoises and other animals, and grow there. Some types of barnacles attach themselves by means of a stalk, or *peduncle,* others by a very strong cement which they secrete and use. The typical barnacles have shells resembling those of molluscs, and for this reason they were classified as molluscs by early zoologists.

Barnacles attach themselves to surfaces at the head end of their bodies, leaving the back end free to draw food into the shell. Barnacles can open the rear end of their shells and pass water through to capture their microscopic

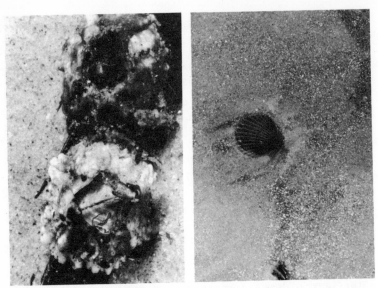

(Left) A barnacle closed in its nearly water-tight shell awaits the return of the tide on this small sliver of piling. These incredible animals feed on the plankton in the water and live for many years. (Right) The shell of a scallop, one of the few molluscs that can actually swim by clapping its two shells or valves together, much as a butterfly flaps its wings.

food. The feathery *cirri*, the broom-like organs with which they sweep the sea water through their shells, are actually much reduced legs, corresponding to the swimming legs of their relatives, the shrimps.

The ridged sunburst pattern of the scallop shell is easy to recognize. The scallop has two halves to its shell and like the clam and oyster is therefore a bivalve. It is able to open the space within the shell and take in water. Then with a quick jerk it can pull the two valves shut and

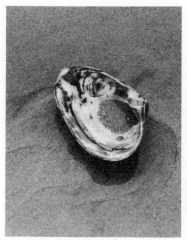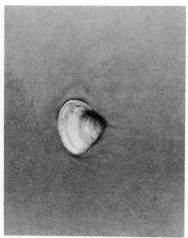

(Left) The inside surface of a surf clam shell. Careful examination of the inside of such shells often reveals tiny invertebrates seeking shelter in the small crannies where the tide has less pull on them. (Right) The shells of quahogs often have bright blue to purple areas, which were made into a kind of money called wampum by the American Indians.

literally squirt itself through the water to a new location. This means of locomotion is actually a sort of jet propulsion. All along the mantle, the outward fringe of tissue lying just inside the shell margins of the scallop, are rows of tiny eyes on stalks. These enable the scallop to watch out for predators.

Another group of bivalves, the mussels, are found nearly worldwide and may live for many years. Mussel shells can be seen in great clusters attached to rocks and pilings but not to moveable objects such as ships. The shells have

MADISON COUNTY ·
CANTON PUBLIC LIBRARY SYSTEM
CANTON, MISS. 39046

The whelk, one of the largest gastropods, drills holes with a rasp-like organ into the shells of clams and oysters and devours the soft-bodied creatures within.

tough, fibrous attachments called *byssus* threads, that hold them to the rocks or pilings. Mussels can break their own byssus threads and move to a new location—they are capable of very slow locomotion, since they possess a muscular foot.

Clams are among the most widely distributed bivalves, ranging from the sand bars in deeper water up to and sometimes even above the middle beach. Hard-shelled clams, or quahogs, have been an esteemed food item in North America since the coming of the American Indians and clam shells have been found at numerous excavated campsites.

The remains of a long, narrow razor clam, whose shell is nowhere near as hard or durable as that of the oyster.

Clams, like mussels, have a muscular foot that can be extruded between the two halves of the shell, enabling the animals to burrow in the sand. Clams are equipped with two tubes or siphons, one for taking in water, with its life-giving oxygen and food particles, the other for expelling waste.

Although the wildlife of the lower beach is totally aquatic and spends most of its life covered by water, a few species migrate to the middle beach to spawn. Also, sick or injured individuals of various species may be stranded on the middle beach.

A large breakwater of heavy pilings and planks stretches into the sea to help increase the beach. Note the shallower water on the left side where the surf has been forced to drop its sand as it sweeps in to the beach.

The lowest beach is constantly covered by the surging of the surf.

Denizens of the Lower Beach

The animals of the lower beach have the vast resources of the sea and its plankton as food, and many are filter feeders, that is, they strain food from water by means of specialized organs.

The strangest of all the creatures of the lower beach is the horseshoe, or king, crab which is properly called a *limulus*. Horseshoe crabs are not crabs at all but belong to an ancient group of arthropods that zoologists put in a class by itself. These animals appear to be more closely related to the arachnids, or spider group, than to the crustaceans, and they show resemblances to such familiar fossil creatures as trilobites. Despite their somewhat fearsome appearance, horseshoe crabs are quite harmless to human beings.

Horseshoe crabs may moult as many as 16 times from egg to adulthood. They gather in great numbers in early summer from May through July and come ashore up to the middle beach, where they lay perhaps a thousand eggs at a time and return to the sea. The limulus has an open circulatory system and a blue-tinted fluid called hemo-

(Left) The underside of the horseshoe or king crab. This is not actually a crab but the last living relative of a species of invertebrate related to the spider which thrived in very ancient shallow seas. (Right) The top or dorsal surface of the king crab.

lymph instead of blood. The sense organs are not understood very well, but there are four eyes—two large ones on either side of the shell, made up of close-packed nerve fibres, and two smaller ones behind the first pair. It is known that the eyes of the limulus can polarize light and this is thought to be an aid in navigation. The heavy spine at the back of the shell is not a tail but an elongation of the top shell, called a *telson*.

The lower beach is the environment of a vast host of bivalves, worms and echinoderms (starfish and their kin),

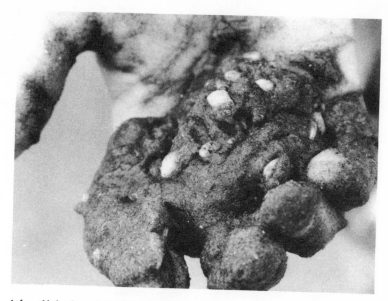

A handful of sand from the lower beach reveals a mass of tiny bivalves and other molluscs hidden just beneath the surface.

A young flounder, partly covered by sand, lurks in waiting for tiny marine worms which it eats.

A large flatfish, the winter flounder, often swims flat on the bottom near the beach to feed. The peculiar adaptation of both eyes on the same side of the head develops as the flounder matures. When hatched from the egg the eyes are on opposite sides of the head like most fish.

which are continually washed in the surf. Not surprisingly, good-sized fishes swim into the lower beach to feast upon the large supply of food. One of the most interesting groups are the flounders and other flatfishes. These fishes hatch and mature in the estuary. As hatchlings of a fraction of an inch in length, they have eyes on each side of the head as in other fishes. However, flatfishes have developed a flattened body suited to living on the bottom. As the hatchling develops, one side of its body becomes the top and the other the bottom. When mature, the

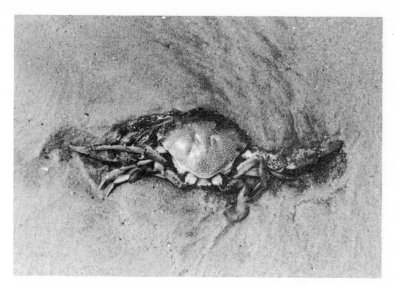

This dead calico crab will soon be devoured by the scavengers of the beach, one of the most voracious of which is another species of crab.

flatfish has both eyes placed on the new topside. This comes about because one eye (called a "celestial eye" because it tends to look up at the sky) migrates over the top of the head. Flatfishes are typically dark on the upper side and white or gray on the lower, which provides protective coloration above and below.

What makes an individual flatfish turn on its side as it grows or why it turns on its right or left side is unknown. In general, each species has a majority of left- or right-handed specimens, but there are always some which revert to the opposite side!

Many types of crabs live along the lower beach where

Coquinas, tiny relatives of the clams, are here magnified several times life size, as they filter the sea water for their food.

This enlarged view of the coquina shows the afferent or intake, and the efferent or exit siphons stuck out of the tiny shell. These siphons pass a constant stream of water and food particles over the filtering organ inside the shell.

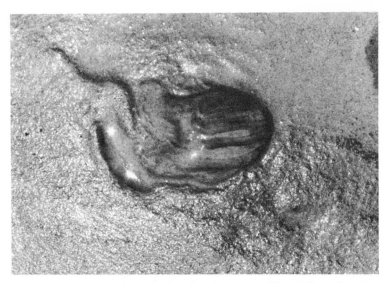

A jellyfish is stranded on the beach. These incredibly delicate inverte-brates have poison cells in their long hanging tentacles, which surround fishes and other small life forms that are swept into the middle of the umbrella-like body and devoured.

they eat and are eaten. But the most numerous residents of the lower beach are the molluscs, especially the bivalves or pelecypods, which are of all sizes, from the tiny coquinas to the large hard-shelled clams or quahogs. All of the bivalves filter seawater by pumping in and out through a set of siphons and a series of gills which extract both oxygen and microscopic plants from it.

A peculiar group of ocean animals almost never found in fresh water is the coelenterates. The most common

In the warmer regions of the lower beach the strange, flower-like anemones thrive. They use their weird tentacles to sting and carry food to their mouths. These are coelenterates, a type of invertebrate animal which has developed in rich variety in the sea but is hardly existent on land.

coelenterates on the lower beach are the jellyfishes. These translucent blue-white animals are almost all circular and cup- or saucer-shaped, with a mouth on the underside and many string-like tentacles equipped with stinging cells. The jellyfish can actually swim upwards through the water by an undulating movement that ripples outward from the middle of the "saucer."

Related to the jellyfish are sessile or non-mobile forms which can easily be mistaken for plants. In fact, they are

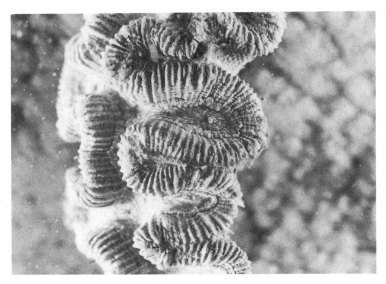

Also a coelenterate, coral grows in colonies, where the individual animals build tiny skeletons out of the minerals they extract from sea water. The whole colony takes on a hard rock-like consistency after years and generations of the tiny animals.

called *Anthozoa,* or flower animals. The most common of these are the sea anemones, which are especially numerous in coastal waters. Sea anemones and jellyfishes can deliver a most unpleasant sting, so beware of them.

The ocean has many other sessile animals of plant-like structure which are not found on land. These creatures usually begin life as eggs or immature free-floating forms. They are then part of the zooplankton (see page 69). As they mature, they anchor themselves to a surface such as rock or to other attached animals and become sessile, which means "fixed" or "non-moving."

While looking like a plant, the common Atlantic Bugula is actually a sessile colony of animals. Each individual organism grows out of the prior one and the whole colony waves in the currents. Bugulas grow on rocks, gravel beds and old wood pilings all along the North Atlantic coast. Magnified 35x.

While they do not move from place to place in the ocean like fishes or shrimps, they are nonetheless in continual movement, fanning and filtering their food from the ocean current. Feeding by the use of waving tentacles, they pass the captured food to a U-shaped but very simple digestive tract. They are widely distributed in most of the salt and fresh waters of the world. However, along the edge of the ocean the sessile animals are usually the smaller, nearly microscopic, species. A careful look with a hand lens or a school microscope will often turn them up, attached to rocks or old pilings.

In and around the lower beach there are also crustaceans

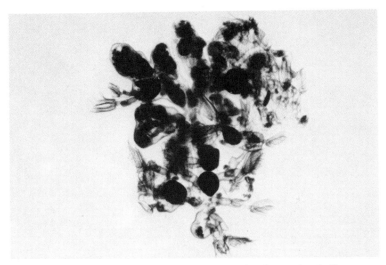

A colony of Bryozoa, a group of sessile animals, shows the shells, tentacles and darker digestive tracts. Magnified 40x.

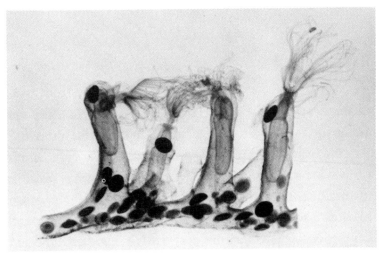

This typical colony of Bryozoa belongs to a simple marine species with only a simple U-shaped digestive tract and no breathing or circulatory organs. Many species of Bryozoa are freshwater organisms and also appear in estuaries. Magnified 30x.

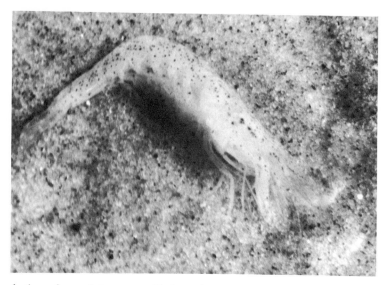

A tiny ghost shrimp magnified to show its many appendages. These delicate-looking creatures survive in the surf where they swim very rapidly.

of many sizes and hues. The shrimps half-swim, half-run along the sand under the water. They can disappear into the soft, water-soaked sands in seconds, and are adapted to eat a wide variety of foods. Many are nocturnal and feed on microscopic animal species, others can feed on larger molluscs, some even devour starfishes. In the same small depressions where shrimps and other crustaceans abound, young fishes are commonplace. These are often immature but completely free-swimming and on a slow migration from the estuarine environment to the open ocean.

One of the many species of spiny crabs is covered with algae which help to obscure it from its enemies and aid in catching its prey.

A large mole crab, better known as a sandbug or bait bug, digs furiously to bury itself in the sand before the next incoming wave. Not true crabs, mole crabs belong to a crustacean group called Amphipoda.

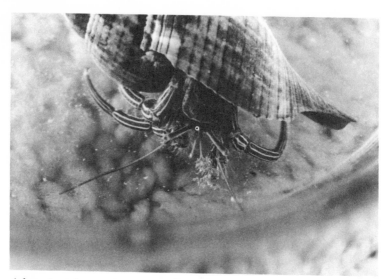

A hermit crab, wearing a cast-off conch shell, slips warily about looking for food. These strange, solitary crabs will disappear into the recesses of their borrowed shells in an instant if startled.

Certainly among the best known and most curious animals of the lower beach are the hermit crabs. Not true crabs, these medium-sized crustaceans have a bare abdomen with no shell covering. To protect this exposed part, each individual seeks the outgrown shell of a mollusc or even some discarded man-made object. Hermit crabs change their homes as they grow, moving to larger quarters, usually another empty shell. Hermit crabs are scavengers and can be attracted by the hundreds with a fish head or other oily meat on a string. Their eyes are mounted on long stalks and can see 360°. The males

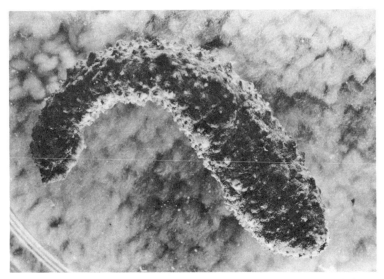
The sea cucumber is another cool water invertebrate, called an echinoderm. It feeds very much like the anemone.

of each species perform a strange mating dance with careful mincing movements, using their extended swimming fins and back legs to hoist their heavy shells clear of the sand. Many crabs of other species prowl along the sands hunting their invertebrate food.

Another group of animals found almost exclusively in ocean water and the lower beach are the echinoderms. These include the sea cucumbers, the various starfishes, the sand dollars and the sea urchins. Each has its peculiar feeding habits. Some sea cucumbers, which are eaten by people in the Orient, can actually expel their internal organs through the mouth as a defensive action to frighten

A tiny starfish, the most common of all echinoderms, pries open a mussel many times larger with the hydraulic-power of its tube-studded feet.

off predators. A new set of organs can then be regenerated.

The sea urchins graze on algae, while the starfish feeds on animal matter. Starfishes crawl about on rocks and muddy bottoms, either scavenging on dead organisms or seeking live prey. They are especially given to feeding on bivalves, whose valves they can force apart with their powerful "arms."

Estuarine Biozones

The estuary is always in marked contrast with the ocean. In its landside there is one continuous zone, in which high and low tide are the only real factors and the extreme from one to the other is nearly indistinguishable. The

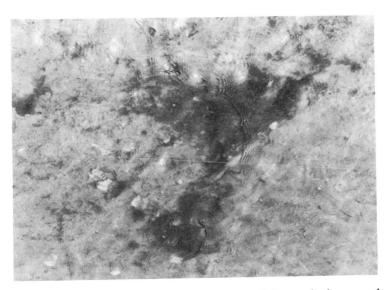

A low-power photomicrograph of an algae mat lying at the bottom of the shallows in the wetlands.

uppermost biozone of the estuary is the undergrowth itself, always acting as an interface zone between the salt marsh and the edge of the woods.

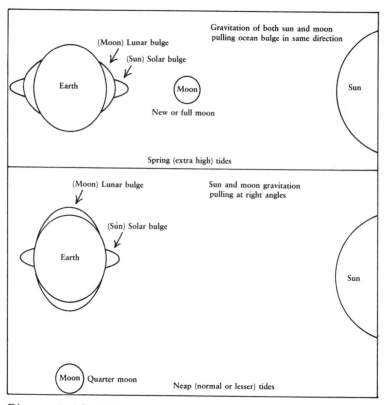

Diagram D. The Tides

Tides, Currents and Waves

The tides of the ocean are caused by the gravitational pull of the moon and, to a lesser extent, of the sun on the vast bodies of water. There are two types of high tides. One, as we have seen, occurs daily at $12\frac{1}{2}$-hour intervals, and is known as the *flood* tide—the low tide corresponding to this is called the *ebb* tide. The second type occurs at the new moon and the full moon, when the moon and sun are aligned so as to produce the highest high tides, which are called *spring* tides. Since spring tides occur every two weeks throughout the year, the term spring refers not to the season but to the idea of rising. During the first and fourth quarter of the moon, the gravitational attraction of sun and moon partially oppose each other and the least of the high tides, called *neap* tides, occur. (Diagram D)

Currents

Tides and their effects and the rotation of the earth produce the complex currents of the ocean. The path of the winds around the earth further complicates these patterns.

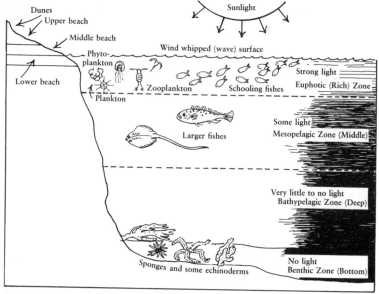

Diagram E. Light Penetration

The mass and extent of coastlines even further influences the height and flow of tides and currents.

The islands in the oceans have very slight tidal extremes, while the narrow bays of Canada and northern Europe have very great tidal changes. Since most of the oceans of the world are over 650 feet (200 metres) deep, there are other factors which come into play. For example, the deeper waters flow in a slightly different direction than the wind-driven surface waters, so that a wide variety of movements may all be going on in one body of water. Diagram E shows the various zones of light penetration of the ocean and the life forms of each zone. While the topmost volume of water receives sunlight, the lower

At high tide, the waves reach in and submerge the middle beach.

A sidewise action of the water at the daily low tide has caused this abundance of shells, algae and bits and parts of sea debris to be laid down along the lower beach.

The receding tide on a smooth lower beach leaves clear water in a slight gully. Such spots are rare along turbulent coasts.

volume where light is meagre contains many nutrient minerals. These two life-sustaining factors mix best at the continental shelves and produce the vast growth of living organisms.

Waves

The familiar waves, which appear as little more than high tide ripples in the estuary make their force felt on the beach. The ocean swells are driven by tidal force against the beach, where the upper ridge of water flows over the reverse current or undertow. This causes the wave to "break" with the familiar white frothy splash and such waves are thus called "breakers."

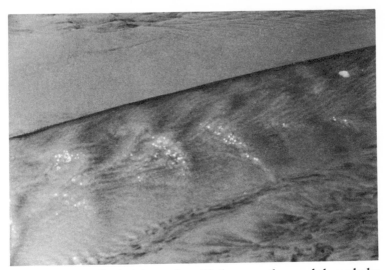

A fast moving gully draining at low tide has carved a canal through the sand.

The ribbed effect of tide on the sand, now left dry at low tide.

Further into the wetlands the tide has less force and merely sweeps the algae plumes ahead as it floods the marsh.

The tides, currents and waves wash the vast piles of shells and parts of plants onto the beach, especially at the spring tide. The constant recession of the low or ebb tide leaves many gullies. These are more often found on the broader, more southern beaches, but do occur as far north as Canada's Maritime Provinces. In the gully, the water warms quickly and there is frequent bacterial breakdown of dead materials. However, as the pressure of the water within the gully increases, the rushing water pouring back into the sea carries away large quantities of sand, cutting channels in the remaining sand as it goes.

A lagoon in the wetlands lies calm at high tide with the algae mats raised above the sand and floating loosely on the water surface.

The estuary has much less wave action and the effect of the tides is reduced so there is little but wind disturbance. However, when the tides flow in through narrow channels or man-made pipes and conduits, a very considerable current can result.

A child has caught a handful of tiny shelled animals, mostly coquinas with just a one-hand sweep through the lower beach sand.

A large tern, cousin to the gull, walks along the beach in search of food.

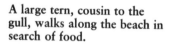

The Cycles of the Ocean

The water of the ocean is recycled in the vast hydrologic cycle, that is, it is evaporated by the sun, falls as rain on the land, is drained in the form of rivers, and returns to the sea. There are many other ocean constituents which also pass through seasonal, monthly or tidal cycles. The most important of all of these constituents are the *phytoplankton* and the *zooplankton*. Plankton consists of organisms which float or drift through the oceans—they have either no ability to swim or a very feeble one. They form the enormous food base upon which the countless invertebrates, fish, birds and marine mammals feed.

Phytoplankton

Phytoplankton are the drifting plants of the ocean. They vary in size from the microscopic diatoms, single-celled plants only a fraction of a thousandth of an inch in size, to the giant kelps which may be over 100 feet (33 metres) in length. The plants of the sea consist of algae of a number of different types. Among the most numerous

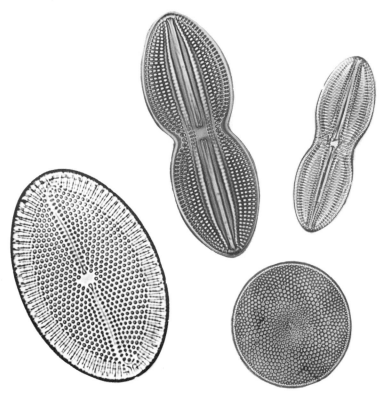

Highly magnified microphotographs of diatoms, the tiny algae which form the very base of the ocean food chain. These minute plants have the ability to extract silicon from sea water and build tiny clear houses or skeletons to support their protoplasm.

algae are the yellow-green ones or *diatoms*. These microscopic, single-celled plants extract silica (the mineral from which glass is made) from the water and construct fine valves or covers so that they live within minute frame-

The brown algae, fucus or rockweed, often break off from their rocky moorings in cool water and float onto beaches with the tiny gas-filled bladders (bead-like parts) acting as floats.

The individual filaments of algae reveal spool-shaped cells.

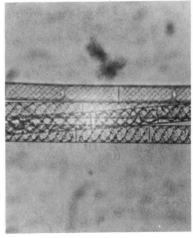

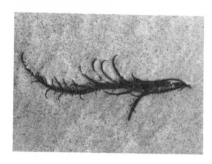

One of the many species of red algae, this frond is tough and fibrous, although feathery in appearance.

works of natural glass. The more visible algae of other species are found everywhere in the ocean currents. They thrive in the estuary as threads in the nearly fresh water and as bubbly scums of light green.

A walk along the beach will reveal many of the ocean species of algae washed up by the tide. Algae are often classed according to their color. The most common is the brown, which is eaten while alive by thousands of species of tiny animals as well as by larger invertebrates. Brown algae are held near the surface by gas bubbles which they take into their systems during life. When dead, brown algae fall to the bottom of the ocean where they are reduced by bacteria. In turn, many species of coelenterates and molluscs devour these bacteria.

Zooplankton

The zooplankton are the free-drifting animal life of the sea. Virtually every drop of beach sea water contains some phytoplankton and small quantities of zooplankton. During their early lives virtually all species of ocean fishes

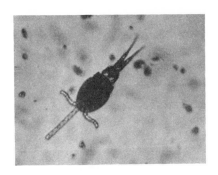

A tiny invertebrate hunts for food in a bare drop of sea water.

and many other species such as the giant squids are zoo-plankton.

Juvenile or Immature Forms among the Plankton

The plankton include vast numbers of plants and animals that are microscopic in size. While most of these are single-celled, some are actually the younger or juvenile stages of much larger and more familiar forms of life. The differences between the young starfish and its 5-armed adult form (some species have more arms), or between the tiny shrimp-like crab *zoea* (crustacean larva) and the adult crab are so great that there is no way of telling that they are related from their appearance. It took nearly a century of close observation and recording by many scientists before the juvenile forms could all be identified.

As we have seen, even the sessile animals often have free-swimming and free-living stages during which the individuals swim away to colonize new rocks or barriers

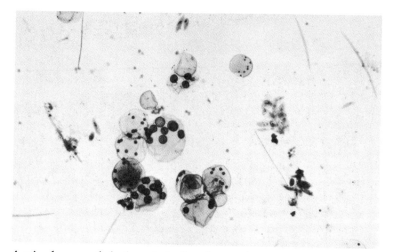

A mixed group of plankton including plants (phytoplankton) and animals (zooplankton). These tiny, mostly one-celled forms drift through the upper currents of the ocean. They are especially rich where nutrients are washed down from the land or well up from deeper water. Magnified 300x.

on new beaches and begin the cycle of settled life all over again. The plankton are one of the most fundamental links in the food-chain of the sea and millions must be produced by each species to ensure their survival and the colonization of new environments. These tiny creatures, which appear defenceless, are so tenacious of life that they are found nearly everywhere in the oceans of the world. Since the sea is so vast, amounting to over 70 per cent of the earth's surface, this must total billions upon billions of individual organisms. This is one of the great mysteries and fascinations of creation.

The phytoplankton and zooplankton increase and decrease in number directly with the availability of the required chemical components. The most important

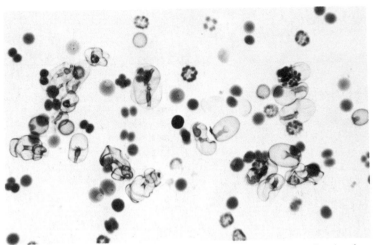

All of these strange-looking animals are different stages in the development of the starfish from egg to the familiar many-armed pattern. These tiny embryonic forms float in the surface plankton. Magnified 120x.

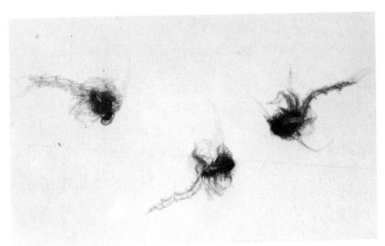

These strange, wispy creatures resemble shrimps. But they are the newly-hatched free-swimming stage of the common blue-claw crab found in the estuary and along the beaches. This microscopic stage is called the zoea and is common among the plankton near the seashore. Magnified 80x.

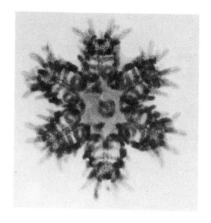

Not a snowflake, but a microscopic young starfish, its six arms developed and the familiar tube-feet reaching out to test the environment. Starfish larvae are found by the millions among the plankton. Magnified 105x.

chemical cycles are: oxygen, carbon dioxide, phosphorus, nitrogen, and silicon. These cycles are shown schematically below.

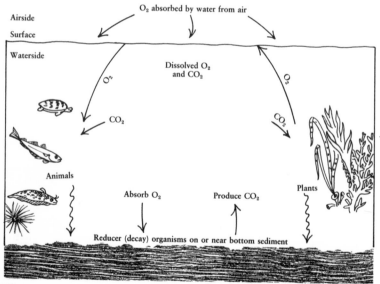

Airside

Surface

O_2 absorbed by water from air

Waterside

Dissolved O_2 and CO_2

O_2

O_2

CO_2

CO_2

Animals

Plants

Absorb O_2

Produce CO_2

Reducer (decay) organisms on or near bottom sediment

Diagram F. Oxygen (O_2) and Carbon dioxide (CO_2) Cycles

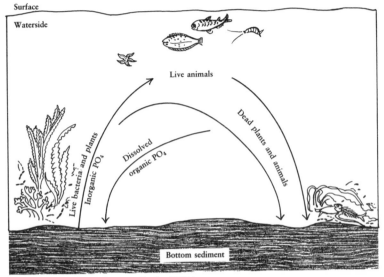

Airside

Surface

Waterside

Live animals

Dead plants and animals

Live bacteria and plants

Inorganic PO₄

Dissolved organic PO₄

Bottom sediment

Diagram G. Phosphorus Cycle (PO₄)

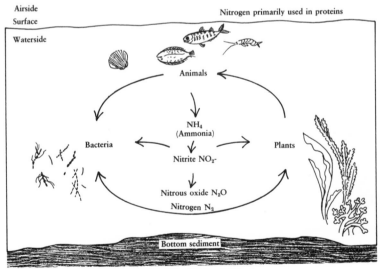

Airside

Surface

Waterside

Nitrogen primarily used in proteins

Animals

NH_4
(Ammonia)

Bacteria

Nitrite NO_2^-

Plants

Nitrous oxide N_2O
Nitrogen N_2

Bottom sediment

Diagram H. Nitrogen Cycle (N_2, NO_2^-, NO_3^-)

77

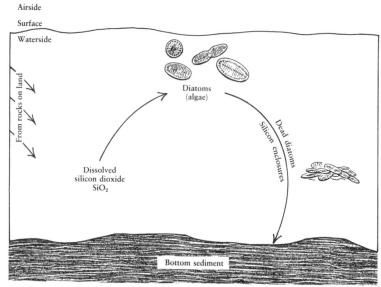

Airside

Surface

Waterside

From rocks on land

Diatoms
(algae)

Dead diatoms
Silicon enclosures

Dissolved
silicon dioxide
SiO_2

Bottom sediment

Diagram I. Silicon Cycle (Si)

A giant sea-going dredge uproots the bottom of the shallow ocean just off the coast. These operations do tremendous damage to wildlife habitats while leaving the ship channels deeper.

The Future of the Ocean Edge

We have seen that the ocean has edges which are enormous and powerful, but also delicate. The actions of human beings and their cities and towns can alter, affect and even poison large areas of the estuary and the ocean. To save beaches, many tourist resorts put in large breakwaters of pilings or rocks which alter the currents. In other places, buildings have been placed right out into the beach area. More severe damage is done by sea-going equipment, which widens channels and churns up vast amounts of debris and sand. But the worst of all are the oil spills that plague coasts around the world. The clean-ups can cost vast amounts of money and result in the deaths of many, many species.

But common littering can be almost as damaging. There are few areas of the earth which can stand cans, bottles, papers, plastic wrappings and similar trash less than the beach. If kept clean and carefully watched, few places are more beautiful or exciting than the edge of the ocean.

Index

574.526
W   White, W.   c. 1

Edge of the ocean

		DATE DUE		

MADISON COUNTY -
CANTON PUBLIC LIBRARY SYSTEM
CANTON, MISS. 39046